MW01242413

# FAITH AND FAVOR
# A WINNING COMBINATION

*10 Principles of Faith to Help Ensure Victory*

*Over Life's Challenges*

*By*
LARRY G. BROWN, SR.

## To My Dearest Wife, Pastor Geneice Brown,

For over four decades, you have stood by my side, guiding and supporting me through the winding paths of life. Your strength, wisdom, and unwavering love have been the cornerstone upon which my successes are built. As both a beacon of faith to our church family and community and the heart of our home, you have continuously inspired me to be better, to dream bigger, and to love deeper. This handbook, a culmination of countless hours and thoughts, is but a small testament to the profound influence you've had on my life. It is to you, my greatest supporter and partner in all things, that I lovingly dedicate this work.

# THE FAITH CODE

## FORWARD

Whenever God wants to do a particular work, He simply calls someone to serve Him in that chosen capacity. In the book of Genesis, God called Adam to do a specific work; one that would lay the foundation for God's purposes on the Earth. He later called Abraham, to establish His prophetic covenant with the chosen people of Israel. On and on, throughout the generations, we see how God chose certain people to achieve the prophetic destiny of humanity. He made them chosen vessels to shift the tides of history, and to conform to God's Kingdom agenda.

All believers are called by God and are given a ministry of reconciliation. All of us are gifted to do specific work for the Lord. All of us have this blessed hope because of Jesus Christ, the hope of glory. Without a doubt, God loves us all equally; however, God sovereignly empowers us according to the particular assignment He has given us.

Another undeniable truth is that there's a higher calling of God, which requires great obedience and sacrifice, plus tremendous responsibility. This kind of calling is about yielding to God's sovereignty; great compassion is needed to guide and position God's chosen elect to fulfill such a great proclamation.

Throughout the generations, God has sovereignly designed these ministry gifts or calling, especially (Apostles), to lead and guide us to colonize the Earth with the life-changing gospel of Jesus Christ. The kingdom's message is the gospel of Jesus Christ, just as taught by His original disciples. This message transcends denominations, colors, and creeds. It is communicated with a premium of love and compassion, with signs following.

To communicate the kingdom's message, God chose the five-fold ministry, apostles, prophets, evangelists, pastors, and teachers for the work of the ministry, and for the edifying of the body of Christ. Ephesians 4:11-13. (KJV)

Recently, God has accelerated His Kingdom mandate by the restoration of the office of the Apostle. The Bible reminds us that God's council shall stand so with fear and trembling we bow to the will of the Lord. The biblical foundation sets the standard and history of the Apostles of Jesus Christ and the great work that was wrought by them.

Today, God is calling humble servants of God like Apostle Larry Brown to continue His great work on the earth as a sanctified builder and repairer of the breach. Roman 1:5 (KJV) reminds us that Jesus Christ is the foundation and source of the apostolic grace given to his chosen apostles.

Despite the gross darkness that covers the earth, God is still shining the "Light". We're so grateful to God for these holy men and women who are steadfast and unmovable, always abounding in the work of the Lord. We're thankful for in advance for God's favor upon Apostle Brown's handbook; such a favor that makes him shine forth brightly in the midst of darkness and hypocrisy.

His handbook, by God's grace, will certainly birth new hope and restoration in the community; we pray that it will cause many souls to seek the Lord afresh also.

This handbook serves as a powerful testament to his calling and elevation. I feel it affirms God's anointing upon this humble soldier of the cross. We pray that the seal of God's glory rests upon Apostle Brown as he serves almighty God on this higher level. In addition, we pray that this handbook encourages all believers that God's council shall stand because it is the Lord's doing and it is marvelous in our eyes Psalm 118:23 (KJV)

Apostle Jerry L. Taylor, Salvation Church of God, Chicago, IL

## WHAT IS THE FAITH CODE?

Where does faith come from? Why do some people seem to have faith and talk about it freely, whereas others struggle? If we don't have strong faith, can we attain it somehow? Here's a call to each Christian, emerging church leaders, and pastors to effectively walk by faith and recognize the favor of God while doing so.

Relevant stories at various stages of my life where I made faith-based decisions that increased my faith and dependence on God and the holy scriptures are well-documented here.

Here's a chronicle of my early years as a Christian, enlisted United States Marine and employment as a Department of Defense support contractor working as provisioning analyst, program analyst, senior logistician, and team lead. Last but not least, twenty-four plus years of pastoral experience.

As usual, the Bible has the answers - to these and more questions about faith. If we look to God's Word, we'll discover His mysteries and realize how God's Kingdom works. The most famous verse addressing this is Romans 10:17 (NASB), *"So faith comes by hearing and hearing by the Word of Christ."* Ponder on that for a minute.

Notice there are two *hearings*. The 'first' is when you hear the Word in the Bible. (Possibly for the first time). The 'second' hearing is when you *really* hear it. It's revealed to you from God's Holy Spirit.

When Jesus taught, He often said, *He who has ears to hear, let him hear.* Matthew 11:15 (NASB). Most likely, everyone in the crowd had physical ears. But that's not what Christ meant. He was talking about spiritual ears. Ears tuned into God and His thoughts.

So, the second hearing is when we hear from God Himself. The Word we have heard with our ears is spoken to us by God's Spirit to our spirit. This is when the Word we heard seems to come alive. We have that "ah-ha" moment. That's when faith in that word is birthed.

Another way of saying this is: It is *revealed*. This is what we call *revelation from God*. When it's revealed, we know at a much deeper level. We haven't just heard it with our ears, we know it. It's ours. That's the simplest way of talking about faith. The more we hear a certain word, the greater the revelation, especially if we allow ourselves to ponder that word. We may speak the word aloud and we think about it as we go about our day.

There's a remarkable story about Lillian Yeomans, a lady who lived during the early 20th century. She had been a medical doctor, serving long hours in an emergency room. To keep up the pace, she had medicated herself with Chloral Hydrate, a highly addictive drug, and had become addicted.

Fewer clinics could help with addiction in those days, so Dr. Yeomans was in terrible shape. She lost her medical license and was in great despair. Until she found Jesus and the Word of God. Lillian Yeomans began to see what the Word said about healing. She read and pondered. Spoke the Words she saw and meditated on them. Through this process, she received healing from the drug addiction.

Yet she couldn't regain her medical license and could never practice medicine again, so she began a new mission. She shared her newfound faith in *Health and*

*Healing*, and other books published by Gospel Publishing Co, Springfield, MO. Dr. Yeomans opened up a house in California where she began to take terminally ill patients. The medicine she dispensed was the Word of God.

Since this was before modern electronics, Lillian used reel-to-reel tapes to play healing scriptures from morning to night. The patients would come in desperate shape, and many of them would leave healed of their disease.

Now and then, Dr. Yeomans would hear shouts and dancing coming from the bedroom upstairs. She would say, "She's got it!" The Word playing over and over had finally penetrated to the point where it became real to the patient. She now had a revelation. She had a Word from God she could cling to. Physical healing often followed.

So, what about you? Is there some area of your life where you need God's hand to move? In healing? In finances? In family problems? Or just to know God better and realize how true He is? How much He loves you? Your key to overcoming these problems and others is to find the scriptures that apply to that area of your life.

With this handbook, there is a list of scriptures you can use. You might also like to find your own. God's Word, the Bible, addresses every area of our lives. Our Father God wants you to have all the benefits paid for by His Son, Jesus, at the cross. Determine in your heart that you are going to find these scriptures and read them, ponder on them, and do it some more—again and again.

At first, they are just words, but as you read them, speak them, and think about them, they become Words, straight from God to you. That's when you develop faith in that area. Your answers are on the way. And in the meantime, you are getting closer to God.

In this handbook, you will learn ten faith-based principles based on many Biblical chapters; they will help you experience a faith-filled life and achieve your goals. Indeed, you will realize that Faith and God's favor in your life is a winning combination!

## LEARNING GOD'S VOICE

As Christians, one of the most important things we can do is to learn to hear God's voice. The ability to discern His voice is essential if we want to live a life He finds pleasing, and if we want to fulfill the purpose He has for us. But learning to recognize God's voice is a lifelong journey, and it requires patience, faith, and humility.

Besides, it's important to approach the process with an open heart and a willingness to surrender to God's will. Different individuals may have different experiences and methods for discerning God's voice. Nonetheless, here are a few general principles that may be helpful:

1. Developing a Relationship: Building a relationship with God through prayer, meditation, and studying the scriptures can create a foundation for recognizing His voice. The more you seek to know and

understand God, the more attuned you become to His voice.

2. Seeking Wisdom: Seek wisdom and guidance from trusted spiritual mentors, religious leaders, or individuals who have a strong connection with God. They can provide insights and teachings that can assist you in discerning God's voice.

3. Silence and Stillness: Set aside regular time for silence and stillness to listen and be open to God's presence. This can be done through meditation, contemplative prayers, or simply finding a quiet space for reflection. Being in a state of receptiveness can help you become more attuned to God's voice.

4. Discernment: Learn to discern between different voices and thoughts. God's voice is often described as gentle and loving, and it's consistent with His teachings. More so, it aligns with virtues such as love, compassion, forgiveness, and truth. It is essential to compare the thoughts or messages you receive with the teachings of your faith and the principles of righteousness.

5. Confirmation: Seek confirmation through prayer and reflection. If you believe you have heard God's voice, take the time to pray for confirmation and guidance. This confirmation may come through a sense of peace, a repeated message, or a deeper understanding that resonates with your spirit.

# ADDITIONAL GUIDANCE:

God speaks all the time, there is no haze on His voice. Therefore, you should hear Him clearly, too. The following is for your consideration so you can know what to look out for.

- o The Word of God, the Holy Scripture is the voice of God in print. You hear Him clearly in it than you would any other way. Meditation on the Word is one sure way to hear God's voice clearly.
- o Furthermore, God speaks when you pray. The voice of God came strong and clear to Jesus when He was praying after His baptism at the river Jordan. When you pray, God interrupts you with His voice. Whether audibly or by just a deep impression in the heart, God's voice when you are praying will often come clear, definite, and very reassuring.
- o God's voice comes through the audible voice of the Holy Spirit. It is God's prerogative and initiative; He chooses the way and manner He speaks to believers at any point in time. But whether audibly or any other way, He speaks to the heart and mind as clearly as possible, and it is left to you to hear Him clearly, too.

  Simply put, no matter how God speaks, the responsibility to hear Him rests on you. God speaks through angels and when He does, the message is clear, concise, and definite. But are you supposed to go seeking God to send an angel to speak with you as He did with Cornelius, Paul, Peter, and Philip in the Bible? The answer is an emphatic NO! They did not seek God to speak to them that way, God made the choice and the call.

So, leave it to the Lord to decide whatever way He chooses to speak to you. But rest assured, if you're in fellowship with the Holy Spirit, you will definitely hear God clearly whenever He speaks to you.

o God still speaks today through prophets and prophecies and when He does it is always clear. Be open to prophecies and you will hear God's voice of clarity showing you the way to go. Despise not prophesyings. The surest way and simple answer to the question of how to hear God's voice is in one word: fellowship.

The real essence of the gospel is fellowship with the Father which is made possible by the Holy Spirit. When you stay in intimate fellowship with the Spirit in prayer, worship, obedience, and study of the word, you will not have a problem hearing God's voice as clearly as possible all the time.

o In worship, the voice of God is heard and heard very audibly, too. If you are a worshipper, a true worshipper of God, one that has mastered the act of worship, God will always speak to you. The Holy Spirit communicates the voice of God. Every time you hear God speak to you, whether audibly or by the inward witness and deep premonitions, that's the Holy Spirit's voice.

By way of introduction, my circuitous route to hearing and walking by faith is as follows:

I was born in Duncan, Mississippi, and raised in Chicago, Illinois, from age four. My parents, Deacon Morris Louis Brown and Missionary Lillie Brown attended Healing Temple Church of God in Christ (COGIC), where I was taught about Christianity as a child and teenager.

I did not want to go to church in my early years. My parents did not have driver's licenses or own a vehicle. At some point, my elder brother, Glen, became the designated driver of a vehicle my parents purchased and transported our family to and from church services. However, when Glen left home, I, the second oldest at age eighteen, became the reluctant driver designated for a vehicle purchased by my parents.

When I look back at that time, I admit that I had a bad attitude toward the church in general. But in early 1977, I attended a revival, accepted Christ, and experienced the presence of the Holy Ghost. This experience removed all doubt in my mind about the existence of God, Jesus, and the Holy Ghost, so much so that I made a vow to serve the Lord for the rest of my life.

I had good intentions, but I didn't keep my vow as planned, like many who stopped attending regular church services. I enlisted in the United States Marine Corps (USMC) on November 8, 1977, at age 19, and attended boot camp at Recruit Depot, Parris Island, South Carolina. Upon graduation, I was assigned Military Occupational Specialist (MOS) 3051 General Warehouseman and stationed at Camp Lejeune, NC (CLNC). In July 1978, I was transferred to the United States Naval Base, Subic Bay, Philippines, for Marine Barracks duty. During this tour of duty and after a successful interview with a promotion board, I was meritoriously promoted to Corporal for exemplary knowledge of and application of USMC basis knowledge and skills and practical application after only serving 16 months in the USMC. Upon completion of my tour of duty, I was ordered back to CLNC at age 21.

Before reporting for duty at CLNC, I went home on leave and, while there, I married Geneice Fondren. Geniece and I met at Healing Temple at ages 11 and 14 and were married on November 11, 1979, at ages 18 and 21, respectively. We lived off base in Jackson, NC, until my first reenlistment and promotion to Sergeant at age 22 after only serving two years and 7 months in the USMC. In 1980, I was transferred to Recruiters School at the USMC Recruit Depot San Diego, CA, and graduated in February 1981.

Subsequently, I was transferred to the 9th USMC Recruiting District, Recruiting Station (RS) in St Louis, MO, and Recruiting Substation Station (RSS) in Ashland,

MO. While there, I was meritoriously promoted to Staff Sergeant after only serving four years in the USMC for enlisting 116 applicants within 12 months. After this achievement and upon my request, I was transferred to RS Chicago, IL, RSS Chicago North Central, in February 1983 at age 25. Afterwards, we had our Berkys on November 3, 1983.

Upon completion of my tour of duty as a Recruiter, I was transferred to Marine Logistics Base (MCLB) Albany, GA, in March 1994, and served as a Career Planner. Then, following my request, my MOS was changed to 2100 Basic Ordnance Marine. Afterward, I was transferred to the USMC Attachment, United States Army Ordnance School, Aberdeen Proving Ground (APG) MD, to attend MOS 2171 Fire Control Instrument Repairer School, which was completed in January 1985.

In June 1985, we had our son, Larry Jr. in Albany, GA. Then, in May 1986, I moved to the USMC Air Station, Kaneohe Bay, HI. After a few years passed, I returned to APG for MOS 2172 Electro-Optical Instrument Repairer School at Schools Company and MCLB Albany for MOS 2175 Small Missile Technician School. I was further transferred to Camp Pendleton, CA, as a Gunnery Sergeant, and served with Electronic Maintenance Company and Ordnance Maintenance Company as an Ordnance Maintenance Chief before deploying to Saudi Arabia in August 1990 in support of Operations Desert Shield/Storm.

I felt an overwhelming need to pray while stationed at Port Al Jubail Saudia, Arabia, because I felt I would be killed and was not at peace. At some point, I was convicted to pray on my knees in front of 15 fellow staff non-commissioned officers in our sleeping tent. This was very challenging for me because I didn't want to pray in front of these men. I wanted to pray in secret, but I finally humbled myself and prayed. While praying, I saw myself in a vision back at Healing Temple COGIC, telling the congregation that as for me and my family, we will serve the Lord. I felt strongly that God was calling me into ministry, so much so that I told the Marines I was responsible for we would survive the war. They asked how I knew, and I replied that I was called to be a Minister. At this point, I had a newfound peace and did not fear for my life again. After serving in Desert Shield Storm, I returned to Camp Pendleton. Unfortunately, not long after my return, my father passed in 1991, and I returned to Chicago for his homegoing services. When I was asked to give a remark during service, I told them that "as for my family and me, we will serve the Lord."

In August 1993—then, I was Master Sergeant Senior Ground Weapons Ordnance Chief, I received orders to go back to MCLB Albany, GA, for duty. Sadly, while I was checking out, my mother-in-law, Lillian Fondren, passed away. Her passing prompted Geneice's desire to return to the Lord. When she mentioned her desires to me, I was logistically minded. So, I planned to visit seven COGIC churches and then select one to join. However, we eventually joined the first church we visited—Walker Tabernacle, COGIC, under Superintendent John Thomas Sr. whose leadership changed our lives. While there, we started attending services regularly but did not hold any offices (i.e., deacon, minister, missionary, etc.).

In June 1996, I returned to APG for duty as a MOS 2181 Senior Ground Weapons Ordnance Chief and Chief Instructor for the 33-week Electro-Optical Ordnance Repairer Course. While there, we attended church services at Refuge Temple COGIC in Aberdeen, MD, where I briefly served as a deacon, and the Evangelistic Church of Deliverance in Harve de Grace, MD, where I sensed the need to answer the call to ministry. Now, because I felt a strong prompting to answer the call of God on my life, I thought to delay it a bit. So, I requested a 3-year family-accompanied tour to Okinawa, Japan. However, things went in the opposite direction. I was given a 1-year unaccompanied tour, which definitely was not my plan.

While I was debating this in my mind, a prophet spoke to me and said what you are about to do will hinder your ministry. So, I heeded the warning and went back to Walker Tabernacle COGIC on February 23, 1997, to preach my initial sermon.

Even when I went back to Walker Tabernacle, my mind was still unstable. But, amid the uncertainty, I heard the

Holy Spirit say to me, "retire and go to the Washington, DC area." The instruction got me into another dilemma because I didn't know anyone in the DC area, and I had not prepared financially for retirement. But, I had to act by faith. Thus, I put in my retirement package, but it was initially denied because I didn't have two years on station and still had orders to Okinawa, 5 Japan. I then requested a waiver of the time of station and cancellation of my accompanied orders to Okinawa. Thankfully, my requests were granted, but I did not have a job lined up. So, I called a Marine stationed at Marine Corps Base Quantico. She told me about our former Commanding Officer at Schools Company MCLB Albany, GA, serving as the Program Manager for Test, Measurement, and Diagnostic Equipment, who interviewed me and gave me my first contactor job as a provisioning analyst.

This offer allowed me to do what God called me to do while still comfortably making earns meet. At first, when the Holy Spirit spoke to me about my calling, it did not seem as though there would be a way out. I was confused and afraid, yet I decided to launch out by faith, and lines began to fall in pleasant places because I obeyed.

That brings us to...

# THE PRINCIPLES OF FAITH SCRIPTURES:

*"If it is disagreeable in your sight to serve the Lord, choose for yourselves today whom you will serve: whether the gods which your fathers served which were beyond the River, or the gods of the Amorites in whose land you are living; but as for me and my house, we will serve the Lord."* Joshua 24:15 (NASB)

1 Kings 19:11-*13 (KJV) "And he said, go forth, and stand upon the mount before the Lord. And, behold, the Lord passed by, and a great and strong wind rent the mountains, and brake in pieces the rocks before the Lord; but the Lord was not in the wind: and after the wind an earthquake; but the Lord was not in the earthquake: And after the earthquake a fire; but the Lord was not in the fire: and after the fire a still small voice. And it was so, when Elijah heard it, that he wrapped his face in his mantle, and went out, and stood in the entering in of the cave. And, behold, there came a voice unto him, and said, What doest thou here, Elijah?*

Psalm 85:8 (KJV)*"I will hear what God the Lord will speak: for he will speak peace unto his people, and to his saints: but let them not turn again to folly."* This verse encourages us to listen to what God is saying to us, for He speaks peace to His people. When we hear His voice, we can be assured that we are on the right path, and we should not turn back to our old ways. Isaiah 30:21 (KJV) says, *"And thine ears shall hear a word behind thee, saying, This is the way, walk ye in it, when ye turn to the right hand, and when ye turn to the left."* God will always guide and direct us in the way we should go. As we learn to hear His voice, we can be confident that He will lead us in the right direction.

# COUNT UP THE COSTS

Walking by faith involves making decisions and taking actions based on one's beliefs and trust in a higher power, such as God. It often requires counting up the cost and considering the potential challenges, sacrifices, and consequences involved. Here are some aspects to consider when counting up the cost while walking by faith:

1. Commitment: Walking by faith often requires a deep commitment to your beliefs and values. It may involve making choices that align with your faith even when they are challenging or go against societal norms or personal desires.

2. Sacrifice: Following a path of faith may involve sacrificing certain things or desires to remain faithful to your beliefs. It could be giving up certain habits, relationships, or material possessions that hinder your spiritual growth or go against your values.

3. Perseverance: Walking by faith can sometimes be difficult and may involve facing opposition, criticism,

or obstacles. It requires perseverance and the willingness to endure through challenging times, trusting that your faith will guide you through.

4. Uncertainty: Walking by faith often involves stepping into the unknown and trusting in the guidance of a higher power-for the believer, God. It may require letting go of the need for complete control and embracing uncertainty, trusting that things will unfold according to a divine plan.

5. Trust and Patience: Trusting in a higher power and having patience are crucial elements when walking by faith. It may require waiting for answers, guidance, or the fulfillment of promises, even when it seems delayed or when circumstances appear contrary to your expectations.

6. Community and Support: Surrounding yourself with a supportive community of likeminded individuals can be essential when walking by faith. They can provide encouragement, accountability, and a sense of belonging as you navigate your faith journey.

7. Joy and Fulfillment: While counting up the cost is important, it's also essential to recognize the joy, fulfillment, and spiritual growth that can come from walking by faith. It can provide a sense of purpose, peace, and a deeper connection to something greater than yourself.

You need to understand that the costs and challenges associated with walking by faith may vary depending on individual circumstances and beliefs. It's a personal journey that requires introspection, prayer, and seeking guidance from your faith tradition or spiritual mentors. This brings us to the point where my "crazy" faith began to show up.

# THE RADICAL FAITH

After receiving my retirement orders which came within four months of my request, I retired from the USMC in October 1997 and purchased our first home in Woodbridge, VA. Then, I started my job in October 1997.

Geneice and I joined another church—Sword of the Spirit Deliverance Ministries, Lorton, VA. The church was under the leadership of Anthony Johnson, who did not only receive me as a minister, but recommended my ordination to the Elders, and appointed me as the Assistant Pastor. Then, in 1998, I was ordained an Elder by the late honorable Overseer, Patricia A. Pringle, founder of Evangelistic Deliverance Ministries Inc, Havre de Grace, MD.

Upon my ordination, Geneice and I began conducting church services in our home in January 2000 which led to the opening of our church, Spirit of Truth Deliverance Church (SOTDC). The church held its first official service in a facility on Easter Sunday, April 23, 2000, and was officially installed by the late Overseer Pringle in April 2000.

At another time, in my journey of faith, I signed a 3-year lease with a commercial property landlord rather than play it safe and use a hotel conference set up for 50 people with coffee and doughnuts for $50 per Sunday on a month-to-month basis. We remained faithful to Sunday school and worship services, Bible study classes, and intercessory prayers. Meanwhile, while we were doing all this, we didn't receive our first member until 9 months later.

One Sunday, as Berkys, was reading the announcements and looking out the window at the empty parking lot, he asked in curiosity, "why am I reading the announcements when there are no people here?" Then I calmly replied, "they will come someday." On another Sunday, I found out that I was struggling in my spirit. Then, I asked Geniece, "Why don't we go somewhere, and I get our praise on?" She replied, "you need to get your praise on here!" Her words were comforting enough to make me realize that I didn't need to go anywhere to raise worship to God. As long as I believed He was there with us—even when no one else was, then, I could raise an altar of praise to Him right where I was.

# PRINCIPLES OF FAITH SCRIPTURES:

In Luke 14:28-30, (NKJV) Jesus says, *"For which of you, intending to build a tower, sitteth not down first, and counteth the cost, whether he have sufficient to finish it? Lest haply, after he hath laid the foundation, and is not able to finish it, all that behold it begin to mock him, Saying, This man began to build, and was not able to finish."* Here, Jesus gives us a practical illustration of what it means to count the cost. Just as a builder must consider the resources needed to complete a project, we must carefully consider what it will cost us to follow Christ.

# DO IT AFRAID!

As Christians, we are called to step out in faith and trust in God's plan for our lives. However, sometimes we may feel afraid or uncertain about what lies ahead. In those moments, we must remember that we can do it afraid - with God's strength and guidance. Here are some steps you can take to support them. **PRINCIPLES OF FAITH SCRIPTURES:**

In Joshua 1:9, (KJV) God encourages Joshua with these words: *"Have not I commanded thee? Be strong and of a good courage; be not afraid, neither be thou dismayed: for the Lord thy God is with thee whithersoever thou goest."* Here, we see that God commands us to be strong and courageous, and He promises to be with us wherever we go. Even when we feel afraid, we can take courage in the fact that God is with us.

In Psalm 27:1, (KJV) David writes, *"The Lord is my light and my salvation; whom shall I fear? The Lord is the strength of my life; of whom shall I be afraid?"* Here, we see that God is our light, our salvation, and the strength of our lives. When we trust in Him, we have nothing to fear.

In 2 Timothy 1:7, (KJV) Paul writes, *"For God hath not given us the spirit of fear; but of power, and of love, and of a sound mind."* This verse reminds us that fear does not come from God. Instead, He gives us the power, love, and sound mind we need to face any challenge. Also, God in says in Isaiah 41:10, (KJV) *"Fear thou not; for I am with thee: be not dismayed; for I am thy God: I will strengthen thee; yea, I will help thee; yea, I will uphold thee with the right hand of my righteousness."* This scripture is a powerful reminder that God is always with us, and He will give us the strength and help we need to face any situation.

Matthew 28:1- 9 (KJV) says that "*In the end of the sabbath, as it began to dawn toward the first day of the week, came Mary Magdalene and the other Mary to see the sepulchre. And, behold, there was a great earthquake: for the angel of the Lord descended from heaven, and came and rolled back the stone from the door, and sat upon it. His countenance was like lightning, and his raiment white as snow: 4 And for fear of him the keepers did shake, and became as dead men. And the angel answered and said unto the women, Fear not ye: for I know that ye seek Jesus, which was crucified. 6 He is not here: for he is risen, as he said. Come, see the place where the Lord lay. And go quickly, and tell his disciples that he is risen from the dead; and, behold, he goeth before you into Galilee; there shall ye see him: lo, I have told you. And they departed quickly from the sepulchre with fear and great joy; and did run to bring his disciples word. And as they went to tell his disciples, behold, Jesus met them, saying, All hail. And they came and held him by the feet, and worshipped him."*

## TRUST GOD'S TIMING

Another thing that is key in the journey of faith is "trusting God's timing." This will often require patience and the ability to embrace the present moment while believing that things will unfold in the right way and at the right time. When you trust God's timing, you will be able to recognize God's favor whether in good or bad times. Now, what is God's favor?

God's favor, often referred to as "divine favor" or "grace," is a concept found in many religious beliefs. It generally refers to the belief that God bestows blessings, protection, and guidance upon individuals or communities. Different religious traditions may interpret and understand God's favor in various ways. Some may see it as material blessings, while others may view it as spiritual growth or inner peace. But it often implies a sense of God's benevolence and positive intervention in one's life. Ultimately, the concept of God's favor is a matter of personal faith and belief.

Now, let me show you how God's timing played out in my life. In August 2002, Geniece and I joined the International Community of Christian Churches under the leadership of Bishop Eugene V. Reeves, Presiding Prelate of the Province of St John and Pastor of New Life Anointed Ministries International (Woodbridge, VA). Then, in August 2007, we returned to the COGIC under the leadership of Superintendent John F. Thomas, Albany District of the Western Georgia Ecclesiastical Jurisdiction (Albany, GA). We continued there until July 2010, when I was appointed Superintendent of the newly formed Apostolic Fire District (AFD) (Northern, VA) by the late Bishop Henderson Spivey, Jurisdictional Prelate, Western Georgia Ecclesiastical Jurisdiction (Atlanta, GA).

In December 2014, the AFD was received into the Virginia Fourth Ecclesiastical Jurisdiction under the leadership of Bishop G. Wesley Hardy, Sr. (Chesapeake, VA). I birthed the Heart for the Community Initiative (H4TCI) after meeting with a group of ministers in January 2017.

# HISTORY OF THE APOSTOLIC FIRE FELLOWSHIP (AFF INT'L)

Over the years, Apostle Brown shared his vision for a network of churches dedicated to a common cause of positively impacting communities and evangelizing every corner of the world, initially under AFD that established as established in July 2010. Its mission was to dynamically transform lives by turning the world upside down with the Gospel by the power of the Holy Ghost Just as the Bible says, *"...These that have turned the world upside down are come hither also"* Acts 17:6 (KJV). At that time, he envisioned multicultural churches, comprised of anointed men and women, committed to proactively seeking lost souls wherever they may be found, and positively impacting communities, locally and abroad.

Through the Heart for the Community Initiative (H4TCI), which he established in January 2017, the mission is to proclaim the Gospel consistently and effectively through community events, informative social media, and social ministry programs. It thereby extends with a vision to be a trusted connection between the needs of diverse communities and the collaborative partners and participants that meet that need.

In September 2019, the AFF Int'l was established as an independent organization and held its first elevation and installation service on January 15, 2022. Acts 17:6 (KJV) says, *"These that have turned the world upside down are come hither drives our mission to dynamically transform lives by turning the world right-side up with the Gospel by the power of the Holy Ghost.* our vision has expanded to be helpers indeed one to another, as described in the parable of the Good Samaritan found in Luke 10:30-37. (KJV)

## PRINCIPLES OF FAITH SCRIPTURES:

Proverbs 3:5-6 (KJV) instructs us to, *"Trust in the Lord with all thine heart; and lean not unto thine own understanding. In all thy ways acknowledge him, and he shall direct thy paths." This verse reminds us to trust in God with all our hearts, and to rely on Him to guide us in all areas of our lives. We must not rely solely on our own understanding, but instead, we must acknowledge God in everything we do, and He will direct our paths.*

*"For still the vision awaits its appointed time; it hastens to the end—it will not lie. If it seems slow, wait for it; it will surely come; it will not delay."* Habakkuk 2:3 (KJV)

*"But they who wait for the LORD shall renew their strength; they shall mount up with wings like eagles; they shall run and not be weary; they shall walk and not faint."* Isaiah 40:31(KJV)

*"Wait for the LORD; be strong, and let your heart take courage; wait for the LORD."* Psalm 27:14 (KJV)

*"There is an appointed time for everything. And there is a time for every matter under heaven."*
Ecclesiastes 3:1(KJV)

*"But do not overlook this one fact, beloved, that with the Lord one day is like a thousand years and a thousand years as one day."* Peter 3:8 (KJV)

*"For I know the plans I have for you, declares the LORD, plans for welfare and not for evil, to give you a future and a hope."* Jeremiah 29:11 (KJV)

## GOD WILL PROVIDE

When you allow God to lead you, and follow His timing, He will provide your needs, and what you need to accomplish His purposes. However, belief in God's provision is often rooted in faith and personal spiritual convictions. Some of these are:

1. Religious teachings: Many religious traditions emphasize the idea that God is a provider who cares for His creation. Sacred texts and teachings often highlight examples of divine provision and promises of God's faithfulness.

2. Historical and personal experiences: Reflecting on personal experiences or stories of others can provide reassurance. Many individuals attribute unexpected blessings, timely assistance, or miraculous interventions to God's provision.

3. Trust and surrender: Trusting in God's plan and surrendering to His will can alleviate anxiety about provision. By acknowledging that God knows our needs and has a larger purpose, individuals find comfort in the belief that God will provide in His own time and way.

4. Prayer and spiritual practices: Engaging in prayer or other spiritual practices can foster a sense of connection with God and provide an avenue to seek guidance and express needs. Many find solace and strength in their spiritual practices, believing that God hears and responds to their prayers.

5. Community support: Sometimes, God's provision can come through the support and care of others. Being part of a community or faith group can provide opportunities for mutual assistance and acts of kindness, reinforcing the belief that God works through people to provide for one another. Depend on God's provisions Receive God-sent help in due season

## Principles of faith scriptures:

*"And my God will supply every need of yours according to his riches in glory in Christ Jesus."* Phil. 4:19 (KJV)

*"For the LORD God is a sun and shield; the LORD bestows favor and honor. No good thing does he withhold from those who walk uprightly."*
Ps. 84:11 (KJV)

*"Now to him who is able to do immeasurably more than all we ask or imagine, according to his power that is at work within us, to him be glory in the church and in Christ Jesus throughout all generations, for ever and ever!"* Eph. 3:20 (KJV)

*"Therefore, I tell you, do not be anxious about your life, what you will eat or what you will drink, nor about your body, what you will put on. Is not life more than food, and the body more than clothing? Look at the birds of the air: they neither sow nor reap nor gather into barns, and yet your heavenly Father feeds them. Are you not of more value than they? And which of you by being anxious can add a single hour to his span of life? And why are you anxious about clothing?* Consider the lilies of the field, how they grow: they neither toil nor spin, yet I tell you, even Solomon in all his glory was not arrayed like one of these." Mt. 6:25-34 (KJV)

*"I pray that out of his glorious riches he may strengthen you with power through his Spirit in your inner being, so that Christ may dwell in your hearts through faith."* Eph. 3:16-17 (KJV)

*"And God is able to make all grace abound to you, so that having all sufficiency in all things at all times, you may abound in every good work."* 2 Cor. 9:8 (KJV)

Remember that in trying to obey God, you will be faced with challenges—from people and situations which may threaten to turn your heart from Him. But you need to be careful so you don't fall prey to these things and turn your heart from God. That said, you have to...

# TUNE OUT NAYSAYERS

As Christians, we are called to follow the path that God has set before us. However, as I mentioned above, sometimes we may face opposition or negativity from those around us. In those moments, we must tune out the naysayers and focus on what God is calling us to do. Tuning out naysayers and maintaining faith can be a challenge, but here are some strategies that can help you in dealing with this situation:

1. Embrace your own beliefs: Have a clear understanding of your own values, beliefs, and goals. When you have a strong foundation in what you believe, it becomes easier to stay focused and confident, regardless of what others say.

2. Surround yourself with positive influences: Surround yourself with people who support and encourage you. Seek out individuals who share similar beliefs and aspirations because their positive energy and support will help you stay motivated and resilient against naysayers. 3. Practice self-affirmation: Remind yourself of your strengths, abilities, and the reasons why you have chosen to walk by faith. Write down positive affirmations and repeat them to yourself regularly. This practice can boost your self-

confidence and provide a shield against negative comments.

3. Seek inspiration: Engage with uplifting and inspiring content such as books, podcasts, or videos that align with your faith and beliefs. These sources can help you stay focused and motivated, reminding you of the reasons you chose this path.

4. Limit exposure to negativity: Minimize your exposure to negative influences and environments whenever possible. This could mean avoiding people who consistently bring you down or reducing your consumption of negative news and social media content. Instead, fill your time with activities and interactions that uplift and inspire you.

5. Develop resilience: Naysayers and criticism can sometimes be unavoidable. Build your resilience by reframing negative comments or criticism as opportunities for growth. Learn from constructive feedback, and let go of unfounded negativity that does not serve your purpose.

6. Stay connected to your faith community: Engage with your faith community or likeminded individuals who can provide support and guidance. Participate in gatherings, meetings, or events that allow you to connect with others who share your beliefs. This network can offer understanding, encouragement, and a sense of belonging.

7. Maintain a positive mindset: Cultivate a positive mindset and focus on the possibilities and opportunities ahead. When you approach challenges with optimism, it becomes easier to persevere and stay committed to your faith, regardless of what others may say.

That said, as believers, we must tune out the naysayers and focus on what God is calling us to do. We can trust in His promises of protection and guidance, and we can have confidence that our labor in His service is not in vain. Remember Paul's urge to us to be steadfast in our faith and always abounding in the work of the Lord 1 Corinthians 15:58. (KJV)

## PRINCIPLE OF FAITH SCRIPTURES:

In Psalm 118:6, (KJV) we read, *"The Lord is on my side; I will not fear: what can man do unto me?"* This verse is *a powerful reminder that when we have God on our side, we have nothing to fear. Even when faced with naysayers or opposition, we can trust in His protection and guidance.*

In Proverbs 16:7, (KJV) we read, *"When a man's ways please the Lord, he maketh even his enemies to be at peace with him."* Here, we see that when we are *following God's will, even our enemies will be at peace with us. This doesn't mean that everyone will agree with us or support us, but it does mean that we can trust in*

*God's guidance and know that He will work things out for our good.*

In Isaiah 54:17, (KJV) we see that, *"No weapon that is formed against thee shall prosper; and every tongue that shall rise against thee in judgment thou shalt condemn. This is the heritage of the servants of the Lord, and their righteousness is of me, saith the Lord."* Here, *we see that God promises to protect us from the weapons and words of our enemies. As His servants, we can trust in His righteousness and know that He will always be with us.*

In 1 Corinthians 15:58, (KJV) Paul writes, *"Therefore, my beloved brethren, be ye stedfast, unmoveable, always abounding in the work of the Lord, forasmuch as ye know that your labour is not in vain in the Lord."* This *verse reminds us that we should be steadfast in our faith and in the work that God has called us to do. Even when faced with opposition or negativity, we can trust that our labor is not in vain.*

## DECISIONS, DECISIONS, DECISIONS!

As Christians, we are usually faced with many choices—both big and small. And, every decision we make has a way of impacting our lives, directly or indirectly. From choosing a career path to deciding where to live to picking a life partner, every choice we make affects our lives and the lives of those around us. Making decisions while walking by faith involves trusting in God's guidance and seeking His wisdom.

Now, here are some key principles to consider when making a decision:

1. Seek God's will: Prioritize seeking God's will above your desires or societal expectations. Spend time in prayer, seeking His guidance and direction. Ask for wisdom and discernment in decision-making.

2. Study and meditate on Scripture: The Bible is a valuable source of wisdom and guidance. Study and meditate on God's Word, allowing it to shape your thinking and provide insights for decision-making.

3. Listen to the Holy Spirit: Develop sensitivity to the leading of the Holy Spirit within you. He can provide guidance, promptings, and peace in making choices aligned with God's will.

4. Trust in God's providence: Believe that God is in control and that He has a plan for your life. Even if you don't have all the answers or a clear roadmap, trust that God will guide you and provide what you need along the way.

5. Surrender personal desires: Be willing to surrender your desires and preferences to God's greater purpose. This requires humility and a willingness to let go of control, trusting that God's plan is ultimately best.

6. Seek counsel and accountability: Seek counsel from wise and spiritually mature individuals who can provide guidance and accountability. They can offer different perspectives and help you evaluate options from a biblical standpoint.

7. Pay attention to peace and intuition: As you consider different options, pay attention to the inner peace and discernment you experience. If a decision aligns with God's will, you may sense a deep peace and conviction in your spirit. Otherwise, your heart may be troubled.

8. Learn from past experiences: Reflect on past experiences where you made decisions by faith. Consider how God guided you and brought about His purposes. Use those lessons to inform your current decision-making process.

9. Step out in faith: Once you have sought God's guidance and considered wise counsel, take the necessary steps forward with faith. Trust that God will be with you, even if the path is unclear or challenging.

10. Embrace the possibility of course corrections: Recognize that even with the best intentions and seeking God's will, you may encounter detours or unexpected turns. Stay open to God's redirection and be willing to adjust your plans if necessary.

# PRINCIPLES OF FAITH SCRIPTURES:

In James 1:5, (KJV) we read, *"If any of you lack wisdom, let him ask of God, that giveth to all men liberally, and upbraideth not; and it shall be given him."* This verse reminds us that when we lack wisdom, we can turn to God in prayer and ask Him for guidance. He promises to give us wisdom generously and without reproach.

In Psalm 25:4-5, (KJV) David writes, *"Shew me thy ways, O Lord; teach me thy paths. Lead me in thy truth, and teach me: for thou art the God of my salvation; on thee do I wait all the day."* Here, we see David's heart for seeking God's guidance and asking Him to teach him His ways. We can learn from David's example and ask God to lead us in truth and teach us His ways as we make decisions.

In Romans 12:2, (KJV) Paul writes, *"And be not conformed to this world: but be ye transformed by the renewing of your mind, that ye may prove what is that good, and acceptable, and perfect, will of God."* This verse reminds us that we should not conform to the world's way of thinking when making decisions. Instead, we should allow God to transform our minds and renew our thinking so that we can discern His good, acceptable, and perfect will for our lives.

# OVERCOMING DISAPPOINTMENTS:

In our walk with God, there will be so many frustrations. However, you can overcome disappointments when you surround yourself with like-minded individuals who can provide strength and perspective during difficult times. Dealing with disappointment caused by other people can be challenging and painful. It's natural to feel hurt, betrayed, or let down when someone fails to meet your expectations. However, there are several strategies you can employ to overcome that hurt and move forward positively:

1. Acknowledge your feelings: Allow yourself to acknowledge and process your emotions.

It's important to validate your feelings and give yourself time to heal. Recognize that it's normal to feel hurt and disappointed when someone lets you down.

2. Adjust your expectations: Assess whether your expectations were realistic in the first place. Sometimes, we place high expectations on others that they may not be capable of meeting. By adjusting your expectations and accepting people for who they are, you can reduce the likelihood of disappointment.

3. Practice self-care: Engage in activities that bring you joy and help you feel better. Take care of your physical, emotional, and mental well-being. This could include exercise, spending time with loved ones, pursuing

hobbies, or practicing mindfulness and relaxation techniques.

4. Seek support: Reach out to trusted friends, family members, or a therapist who can provide a listening ear and support. Sharing your feelings and experiences with someone you trust can help you gain perspective and process your emotions.

5. Communicate assertively: If the disappointment stems from a specific incident or behavior, consider having an open and honest conversation with the person involved.

Clearly express how their actions affected you and listen to their perspective as well. Effective communication can help resolve misunderstandings and provide an opportunity for growth.

6. Practice forgiveness: Forgiveness is not about condoning the hurtful actions or forgetting what happened. It's about freeing yourself from the negative emotions associated with disappointment. Forgiving someone can help you let go of the pain and move forward with your life.

7. Focus on personal growth: Use the experience as an opportunity for personal growth and self-reflection. Reflect on what you have learned from the disappointment and how you can apply that knowledge in future relationships or situations. Focus on your own

goals and aspirations to regain a sense of control and purpose.

8. Surround yourself with positivity: Surround yourself with supportive and positive influences. Spend time with people who uplift you, engage in activities that inspire you, and consume content that promotes positivity. Creating a positive environment can help you heal and regain confidence.

Remember, healing takes time, and everyone's journey is different. So, be patient and kind to yourself as you navigate the process of overcoming hurt and disappointment. My greatest disappointments came from people I loved, supported, and empowered. It became obvious they didn't appreciate the value of my counsel and experience.

## PRINCIPLE OF FAITH SCRIPTURES:

In Psalm 42:5, (KJV) the psalmist writes, *"Why art thou cast down, O my soul? and why art thou disquieted in me? hope thou in God: for I shall yet praise him for the help of his countenance." This verse reminds us that even in times of disappointment, we can still have hope in God. We can trust that He is with us and that He will help us through whatever we're facing.*

In Isaiah 41:10, (KJV) God says, *"Fear thou not; for I am with thee: be not dismayed; for I am thy God: I will strengthen thee; yea, I will help thee; yea, I will uphold thee with the right hand of my righteousness." This verse is a powerful reminder that God is always with us, and He will give us the strength and help we need to overcome any disappointment.*

In Romans 8:28, (KJV) Paul writes, *"And we know that all things work together for good to them that love God, to them who are the called according to his purpose." This verse reminds us that even our disappointments can be used for good in God's plan. He can take our struggles and turn them into something beautiful.*

In Philippians 4:6-7, (KJV) Paul writes, *"Be careful for nothing; but in every thing by prayer and supplication with thanksgiving let your requests be made known unto God. And the peace of God, which passeth all understanding, shall keep your hearts and minds through Christ Jesus." This verse encourages us to bring our disappointments to God in prayer and thanksgiving. When we do, He will give us a peace that surpasses all understanding.*

## WALK BY FAITH

Every believer has been called to walk by faith and not by sight. This means trusting in God's plan for our lives even when we cannot see the path ahead clearly. When you find yourself wanting to give up on your walk with God, it can be helpful to remember the following strategies:

1. Reflect on your purpose: Reconnect with the reasons you chose to walk by faith in the first place. Remind yourself of the values, beliefs, and goals that inspired you. Reflect on the positive impact your faith has had on your life and the lives of others. By revisiting your purpose, you can regain clarity and motivation.

2. Seek support: Reach out to your faith community, close friends, or mentors who can offer guidance and support during challenging times. Share your struggles and concerns with them, and allow them to provide encouragement, advice, and prayer. Surrounding yourself with a supportive network can help you regain strength and perspective.

3. Find inspiration: Seek out sources of inspiration that resonate with your faith. This could include reading sacred texts, listening to uplifting sermons or podcasts, or engaging with spiritual literature. These resources can reignite your passion, renew your perspective, and remind you of the strength and resilience that faith can bring.

4. Practice self-care: Take care of your physical, mental, and emotional well-being. When you're feeling overwhelmed or close to giving up, it's crucial to prioritize self-care. Engage in activities that bring you joy, relaxation, and peace. This could include exercising, practicing mindfulness or

meditation, spending time in nature, or pursuing hobbies that recharge you.

5. Break it down: If your journey feels overwhelming, break it down into smaller, manageable steps. Set achievable goals and focus on taking one step at a time. Celebrate your progress along the way, no matter how small it may seem. This approach allows you to build momentum, stay motivated, and see tangible progress.

6. Embrace adversity as growth: View challenges and setbacks as opportunities for growth and learning. Difficulties can strengthen your faith and character, providing valuable lessons that shape you into a stronger individual. Embrace the idea that struggles are part of the journey and that overcoming them can lead to personal transformation.

7. Renew your faith through prayer or meditation: Take time to connect with your faith through prayer, meditation, or contemplation. These practices can help you find inner peace, guidance, and a renewed sense of purpose. Allow yourself to surrender your worries and doubts, seeking guidance from a higher power.

8. Seek professional help if needed: If you find yourself constantly overwhelmed, experiencing deep despair, or struggling with persistent negative thoughts, consider seeking support from a mental health professional or counselor. They can provide

guidance, tools, and strategies to help you navigate challenges while maintaining your faith. Walking by faith is a journey that may have its ups and downs. During challenging times, it's important to be patient with yourself, seek support, and remain open to the lessons and growth that can come from persevering.

# PRINCIPLE OF FAITH SCRIPTURES:

In 2 Corinthians 5:7, (KJV) *Paul writes, "For we walk by faith, not by sight." This verse is a powerful reminder that as believers, we are called to trust in God's plan for our lives even when we cannot see the path ahead clearly. We must have faith that He will guide us and lead us in the right direction.*

In Hebrews 11:1, (KJV) we read, *"Now faith is the substance of things hoped for, the evidence of things not seen." This verse reminds us that faith is a substance - something real and tangible that gives us hope for the things we cannot yet see. We can trust in God's promises even when they have not yet come to pass.*

In Proverbs 3:5-6, (KJV) we read, *"Trust in the Lord with all thine heart; and lean not unto thine own understanding. In all thy ways acknowledge him, and he shall direct thy paths." This verse encourages us to trust in God with all our hearts and to acknowledge Him in all* our ways. When we do, He will direct our paths and guide us in the right direction.

In Matthew 14:29-30, (KJV) we read about Peter walking on water: "And he said, Come. And when Peter was come down out of the ship, he walked on the water, to go to Jesus. But when he saw the wind boisterous, he was afraid; and beginning to sink, he cried, saying, Lord, save me." This story is a powerful reminder that when we keep our eyes on Jesus and trust in Him, we can do the impossible. But when we focus on the storms of life, we can become afraid and lose our faith.

Mark 9:23 (KJV) "Jesus said to him, If you can believe? All things are possible for one who believes."

Matthew 17:20 (KJV) "Truly I tell you, if you have faith as small as a mustard seed, you can say to this mountain, 'Move from here to there,' and it will move. Nothing will be impossible for you."

Matthew 21:22 (KJV) "And whatever you ask in prayer, you will receive, if you have faith."

James 1:6 (KJV) "But when you ask, you must believe and not doubt, because the one who doubts is like a wave of the sea, blown and tossed by the wind."

James 1:3 (KJV) "Because you know that the testing of your faith produces perseverance."

1 Timothy 6:11 (KJV) *"But you, man of God, flee from all this, and pursue righteousness, godliness, faith, love, endurance and gentleness."*

## YOU ARE A TESTIMONY:

As Christians, we are all living testimonies of God's love and grace. Consequently, our lives can be a powerful witness to those around us, demonstrating the transformative power of Christ. And one of the ways we can do hag is by encouraging someone in their faith journey—which can be a powerful way to support and uplift them. Wondering how to make this happen? Here are some ways you can do that:

1. Active listening: Take the time to truly listen to people's experiences, doubts, and questions without judgment. Show genuine interest and empathy, allowing them to express themselves freely. By actively listening, you create a safe space for them to share and feel understood.

2. Share your journey: Share your own experiences, struggles, and victories in your faith journey. When you are open and transparent about your own experiences, you can encourage and let them know that they are not alone in their struggles. Authenticity can foster a sense of connection and inspire them to continue on their path.

3. Provide reassurance:  remind them that doubts and questioning are natural parts of a faith journey. Let them know that it's okay to have questions and that it is through seeking answers that growth and deepening of faith can occur. Emphasize that their journey is unique and that everyone experiences faith differently.

4. Offer resources: Recommend books, podcasts, sermons, or other resources that have been influential in your own faith journey. These resources can provide them with inspiration, guidance, and different perspectives that may resonate with them.

5. Pray for and with them:  Pray for them and their faith journey in your closet. If they are comfortable with it, you can also hold hands and pray with them. Prayers can provide comfort, strength, and a sense of spiritual support. Be mindful of their beliefs and practices to ensure your approach aligns with their faith tradition.

6. Be a supportive presence: Be there for them consistently and unconditionally. Show up during their highs and lows, providing support, encouragement, and a listening ear. Let them know that they can rely on you for guidance, prayer, and encouragement throughout their faith journey.

7. Celebrate milestones: Acknowledge and celebrate their milestones, no matter how small they are. Recognize their growth, achievements, and steps of faith. Celebrating these moments can reinforce their

progress and give them the motivation to keep moving forward.

8. Respect their boundaries: Understand and respect their boundaries regarding their faith journey. Everyone's journey is unique, and it's important to honor their choices, doubts, and decisions. Avoid pushing your own beliefs or agenda onto them. Instead, focus on providing support and encouragement. Remember that because everyone's faith journey is personal, what works for one person may not work for another. By offering genuine support, understanding, and encouragement, you can create a positive and empowering environment for someone to navigate their own faith journey.

## PRINCIPLE OF FAITH SCRIPTURES:

In Matthew 5:16, (KJV) Jesus says, *"Let your light so shine before men, that they may see your good works, and glorify your Father which is in heaven."* This verse reminds us that our lives should be a shining example of God's love and grace. We can demonstrate this through our good works and the way we treat others.

In 1 Peter 2:9, (KJV) Peter writes, *"But ye are a chosen generation, a royal priesthood, an holy nation, a peculiar people; that ye should shew forth the praises of him who hath called you out of darkness into his marvellous light."* This verse reminds us that as believers, we are a chosen and holy people. We have been called out of darkness into God's marvelous light, and our lives should reflect that transformation.

In 2 Corinthians 3:2-3, (KJV) Paul says, *"Ye are our epistle written in our hearts, known and read of all men: Forasmuch as ye are manifestly declared to be the epistle of Christ ministered by us, written not with ink, but with the Spirit of the living God; not in tables of stone, but in fleshy tables of the heart."* This is a reminder that our lives are like letters, read and known by all those around us. As we live out our faith, we become a living testimony of Christ's love and grace. My prayer is that this handbook be used as a guide to help strengthen your faith on your daily life. As an added bonus, I have added a few scriptures and short lessons in the latter pages to help you along your journey. Please feel free to reference these lessons and guides as you continue to build upon your faith. God's grace and peace be unto you!

# THE FAITH CODE:
## SCRIPTURE REFERENCES

## SCRIPTURE PRAYERS AND PROMISES

Do you have any scriptures that resonate with your life and journey of faith? Having Bible passages that always speak to your life at any time can help build your faith in God. This is why I made a list of scriptures that may help you—especially if you are just starting.

**Read Galatians 3:13-14 (NASB)** *"Jesus became a curse for us that the blessings of Abraham might come to us who are in Christ Jesus. Then the blessings are listed in.*

**Read Deuteronomy 28:1-14**. (NASB) Although **the rest of Deuteronomy 28 lists the curses, reading those p**ronouncements does not mean that those are not God's will for you. Jesus paid the price for you to walk in blessings and not curses. This gives you faith to speak against anything which you know is not God's will.

**Deuteronomy 28:13 (NASB)**
*"And the Lord shall make you the head and not the tail, and you only shall be above, and not underneath if you will listen to the commandments of the Lord your God, which I charge you today, to observe them carefully."*

**Psalm 1:1-3 (NASB)**

*"How blessed is the man who does not walk in the counsel of the wicked, nor stand in the path of sinners, nor sit in the seat of scoffers. But his delight is in the law of the Lord, and in His law he meditates day and night. And he will be like a tree firmly planted by streams of water, which yields its fruit in its season. And its leaf does not wither, and in whatever he does, he prospers."*

**Psalm 91:1(NASB)**

*"He who dwells in the shelter of the most high, will abide under the shadow of the Almighty."*

**Psalm 91:11-16 (NASB)**

*"For He will give His angels charge concerning you, to guard you in all your ways; They will bear you up in their hands, lest you dash your foot against a stone. You will tread upon the lion and cobra, the young lion and serpent you will trample down. And the Lord says: Because he has loved Me, therefore I will deliver him. I will be with him in trouble; I will rescue him and honor him. With long life I will satisfy him, and let him behold My salvation."*

**Isaiah 53:5 (NASB)**

*"For He was pierced through for our transgressions, He was crushed for our iniquities; the chastening for our wellbeing fell upon Him, And by His scourging we are healed."*

## Isaiah 54:14 (NASB)

*"In righteousness you will be established; You will be far from oppression, for you will not fear; and from terror, for it will not come near you."*

## Isaiah 54:17 (NASB)

*"No weapon that is formed against you will prosper; and every tongue that accuses you in judgment you shall condemn. This is the heritage of the servants of the Lord, and their vindication is from Me, declares the Lord."*

## Ephesians 1:16-19 (NASB)

*"I do not cease to give thanks for you while making mention of you in my prayers that the God of our Lord Jesus Christ, the Father of Glory, my give to you a spirit of wisdom and revelation in the knowledge of Him. I pray that the eyes of your heart may be enlightened, so that you may know what is the hope of His calling, what are the riches of the glory of His inheritance in the saints, and what is the surpassing greatness of His power toward us who believe."*

## Ephesians 3: 14-21 (NASB)

*"For this reason, I bow my knees before the Father, from whom every family in Heaven and on earth derives its name, that He would grant you, according to the riches of His glory, to be strengthened with power through His Spirit in the inner man. So that Christ may dwell in your hearts through faith, and that you, being rooted and grounded in love, may be able to comprehend with all*

*the saints what is the breadth and length and height and depth, and to know the love of Christ which surpasses knowledge, that you may be filled up to all the fullness of God. Now to Him who is able to do exceeding abundantly beyond all that we ask or think, according to the power that works within us, to Him be the glory in the church and in Christ Jesus to all generations forever and ever. Amen"*

## Colossians 1:9-12 (NASB)

*"For this reason also, since the day we heard of you, we have not ceased to pray for you and to ask that you may be filled up to all the knowledge of His will in all spiritual wisdom and understanding, So that you may walk in a manner worthy of the Lord, to please Him in all respects, bearing fruit in every good work and increasing in the knowledge of God; Strengthened with all power, according to His glorious might, for the attaining of all steadfastness and patience, Joyously giving thanks to the Father, who has qualified us to share in the inheritance of the saints in light."*

## I John 4:4 (NASB)

*"You are from God, little children, and have overcome them; because greater is He that is in you than he who is in the world."*

Did you find them helpful? Now, having given you scriptures to build your faith in God's promises for your life, there are also many Bible references for instruction;

to give you faith to overcome any problem you have, and they are listed below.

### For Marriage

Genesis 2:24, Proverbs 5:18, Proverbs 21:1, Proverbs 31:28, Ephesians 5:22-23; 25, Romans 15:5-7

### For Children

Deuteronomy 28:4a Deuteronomy 30:6 Psalm 112:2 Proverbs 11:21, Isaiah 44:3, Isaiah 54:13, Isaiah 59:21 Isaiah 61:9, Jeremiah 31:16-17, Ephesians 6:1-4

### For Healing

Proverbs 4:20-22, Joshua 21:45, Romans 8:11, II Corinthians 1:20, Exodus 15:26, Matthew 8:2, Deuteronomy 7:15 Psalm 103:1-5, Psalm 91:16 Isaiah 53:5 Jeremiah 30:17 Mark 11:24 John 10:10

### For Finances

Deuteronomy 8:6-9, Deuteronomy 8:18, Deuteronomy 11:10-12, Deuteronomy 28:8, 12  Psalm 1:1-3, Psalm 112:3 Philippians

# FIND THE WORD AND KEEP IT

The Bible is not just another random literature book that you can decide to read only when you have a particular problem or need answers to some subject questions. It contains God's word for your life and destiny. Even though sometimes God does not speak in clear terms, the Holy Spirit can interpret them to you.

For instance, when we look at the teachings of Jesus, we often see Him speaking in Parables. Stories that demonstrate the truth of God's Kingdom. When he paints these pictures, we can understand better how God's principles work through the Help of the Spirit. Through His help, we can get those ah-ha moments – and apply the knowledge to our lives.

As I look back over my life, I realize that clearly, I was not the best-qualified applicant in most cases, yet was given above-average annual pay increases and promotions from my supervisors over a twenty-two period. All these happened because I subjected myself to digging out God's word for my life and allowing His Spirit to guide my heart in everything I did.

In talking about God's word and parables, what many people call the "Granddaddy" of all parables is found in Mark 4, Matt 13, and Luke 8. We'll be looking at each of them to see what Jesus said and how His disciples responded.

 Mark 4:3-8 (NIV) account. *"Listen! A farmer went out to sow his seed. As he was scattering his seed, some fell along the path, where birds came and ate it up. Some fell on rocky places, where it did not have much soil. It sprang up quickly, because the soil was shallow. But when the sun came up, the plants were scorched, and they withered because they had no root. Other seed fell among thorns, which grew up and choked the plants, so that they did not bear grain. Still other seed fell on good soil. It came up, grew, and produced a crop, some multiplying thirty, some sixty, some a hundred times."*

The disciples wanted to know what all of this meant, and Jesus told them exactly what it meant because He was physically with them.

Now, this parable can be like a measuring rod for all of us. Just as we see in the above scripture, our lives are fluid. We can be full of faith at one moment, and the next week be full of worry. Or we can have great faith in certain aspects of our lives, and not so much in others. Sometimes, these things happen because a seed has not been sown in our lives. That brings us to...

## THE SEED, THE SOIL, AND THE FARMER

Jesus said in Mark 4:14 (NIV) that *"The farmer sows the Word."* The seed is the Word of God, and it is sown into our hearts. Good enough, you can't sow a seed on just any soil. If you have ever done any gardening at all, you know how significant the soil is—it must be fertile soil so that the seed can germinate and grow well.

This reminds me of Marian's family who moved into an old house with a courtyard. In the middle of the courtyard, there were six rose bushes—I should say, pitiful rose bushes. They were scraggly and didn't have many leaves, and most of them did not bloom. They looked like they were going to die, and they had looked like that for years.

The people who had owned the house previously had said, "Those roses haven't done very well. They don't get enough sun." Yet Marian noticed that the sun was beaming on that courtyard almost all day. One day, she decided to put a brick walk in the courtyard and started digging up the roses. To her surprise, the ground was so hard, she could hardly dig. The soil was hardened clay and couldn't have possibly provided many nutrients.

The rose problem wasn't the sun! It was the soil. Marian and her husband started adding richer dirt and fertilizer to the courtyard soil. The plants they planted grew abundantly – and the courtyard became the most beautiful place in the landscape! As Marian applied that newfound knowledge to her life, she realized that when things weren't going very well, she needed to check the soil—in other words, check her heart.

In the parable of Jesus, the soil represents the heart. The spiritual heart of mankind, and the seed is God's word. In the parable, you might have noticed that it was the same farmer throwing the seed, and it was the same seed being thrown everywhere. So, who is the farmer? The farmer is the Lord casting the seed into our lives. The seed is the Word of God, and the soil is the spiritual heart of man. In this parable, the type of soil is what determines the crop. The same seed, thrown by the same farmer, produced everything from nothing at all to a bountiful crop. Depending on the soil into which it was planted.

## TYPES OF SOIL

The different types of soil here refer to the different hearts. In understanding the types of hearts we have, we can decide to be those with an abundant harvest of God's blessing and purpose in our lives.

## THE STONY HEART

The first type of heart is the stony heart. This can be seen in Mark 4:14–15 (NIV) *"The farmer sows the Word. Some people are like seed along the path where the word is sown. As soon as they hear it, Satan comes and takes away the word that was sown in them."* Many people usually think that this passage is not for them. They feel they are not the ones who cast away the word immediately, and their heart is a fertile ground.

The truth is, Just as a garden can have stony places in it, so can your heart. Your heart might be soft and pliable for God's Word in certain truths, but very hard in others. You might be a believer in Jesus, but have certain areas which almost annoy you when they are approached. How do you react when you hear about healing? Prosperity? Speaking in tongues? God's love for all of mankind?

If you cannot accept all truth in God's word, then you need to spend some time with the Father, and let Him speak to you about your heart. Note that this is a self-assessment, not a test someone else is giving you to see what you believe. If there are areas where you sense the Holy Spirit is nudging you, spend some time in the Word meditating on these things. Nobody knows it all or lives it all. There is much more to God's Kingdom plans than any of us have experienced.

The more we receive and believe from the Word, the more we can in our lives and in our families. So, be humble enough to ask your heavenly Father to show you where your heart is hard. Ask Him to make your heart pliable so that you can receive all that He has.

On the other hand, if you have never received Jesus, now is the time to do it. Ask Him to come into your life. To be your Savior and your Lord. He's willing and ready to receive you as a child of God. That's the first step to having your ears open to the truth. When this is done, the Holy Spirit will help you to break up the fallow ground of your heart, and receive the Word completely and grow in faith.

## THE ROCKY SOIL

This is the second type of heart the Bible tells us about. Initially, we talked about the stony heart which receives nothing from God. Now, let's see what Jesus says about the Rocky heart in Mark 4:16 "*In a similar way, these are the ones on whom seed was sown on the rocky places, who, when they hear the Word, immediately receive it with joy. And they have no firm root in themselves, but are only temporary. Then when affliction or persecution arises because of the Word, immediately they fall away."*

We all know people like this. They are blown everywhere by the wind. One day they are up. One day they are down.

It's interesting that when the soil is rocky, it doesn't have depth. So, people are as quick to receive the word as they are to fall away from it. Now, you may be asking, what makes for not much depth of soil? What are the rocks? How can we avoid this dilemma?

First, let's back up for a moment. There is something that we must notice here. Earlier we commented that in this parable, the farmer is the same – tossing out seed where he walks. The seed is also the same, being planted in many places and in many types of soil. What makes the difference in the production is the soil, and the soil represents the different types of spiritual hearts in people.

You can have a hard heart, not wanting to hear anything from God. Or you can have a soft, pliable heart – wanting to hear from God and wanting to learn how to apply what you hear. Each person is responsible for his or her own heart. So, when we come to the rocky soil – with lots of rocks and not much soil, we have to ask "Why? What's the cause of this problem?" This soil isn't quite like the wayside, but it hasn't been tilled properly. It's loaded with rocks. Hard places, like a semi-hard heart. This type of heart doesn't have much conviction one way or another. No strong principles. Nothing strongly rooted in that heart.

So, when someone shares the Word that Jesus died for their sins, they say, "Great! That sounds wonderful." But then when someone else makes fun of them for their newfound belief, this person backtracks and decides maybe not, and they begin to doubt their faith in Christ.

This brings us to the story of Jane and Joan who were sisters and loved to share lifestyle ideas. Well, one day Joan read about some great recipes which would help with nutrition and weight loss. She was excited and began to make a lifestyle change. Joan began to buy whole fresh foods. She shied away from preservatives, overly processed food, and sugar. She also joined a gym and began to tone up her muscles and lose weight. As always, Joan shared her new ideas with Jane, and Jane also got excited about it.

However, Jane didn't change her diet or her lifestyle. She thought that was a great idea, but never applied any of it. Soon another friend began to share a different weight loss program. This one didn't include whole foods, but shakes and capsules which were supposed to burn fat quickly. According to this friend, this new diet was the greatest one ever, and Jane fell for that. In fact, the new friend made fun of the tried-and-true healthy eating and exercise. Why go to all that trouble when you can just take these pills? And eat anything you want.

Now, this picture is like the rocky-hearted person. Jane quickly accepted Joan's ideas, but didn't apply them. The she was ready to quickly be persuaded that there was a better way. (My guess is that Jane didn't really apply this one either). If you want to benefit from a program, you have to partake of it yourself. Whether it's food or the Word of God. Just to hear about it and get excited, without truly receiving it into your life, will never produce anything. That's like the person with the stony heart. When you don't have a strong conviction, you can be easily swayed when persecution or affliction comes your way.

Non-Christian friends could start to mock you. You might not be invited to certain events. You could feel yourself isolated. Spiritual attacks might come also. You may find your mind being bombarded with negative thoughts. Fears about your life, your family, or your finances may come. But, you don't have to give in. You have to fight thoughts condemning you for whether for your past mistakes or anything.

The best way to overcome a rocky heart is to persist, regardless of how you feel. If you can't handle it, you can ask some faithful friends to pray for you. Also, don't fail to keep planting that Word into your heart. Keep reading it and saying it. Even if you aren't sure, speak those words aloud. Continue to plant that seed of the Word into your heart, regardless of how you might feel. And regardless of the persecution. What you will find is that you will begin to believe it more and more.

Moreso, you need to know that when you are receptive, anything you plant in your heart will grow. Mark 4:26 (NASB) says *"And He (Jesus) was saying, the Kingdom of God is like a man who casts seed upon the soil; and he goes to bed at night, and gets up by day, and the seed sprouts and grows – how, he himself does not know. The soil produces crops by itself; first the blade, then the head, then the mature grain in the head."*

Anything your heart receives will germinate, whether it's good Word or bad thoughts. That's why it's a good idea not to ponder on negative things because they will definitely affect you.

That said, plant God's Word, and continue to live it out daily—whether you feel it or not; believe it; or not. As you continue doing this, your faith will begin to take its roots and mature. Even though the process might take time, don't stop planting and you will see a beautiful result.

In building up faith, people will come to talk you out of what you know with your mind to be true from God's Word. But, Don't give in to what they say. Do you know why? Someday, you will know beyond a shadow of a doubt that God's word concerning you is true. Your spirit will confirm what you will see with your eyes and hear with your ears, and your faith will be established.

# THE WEEDY SOIL

The third type of soil (heart condition) could apply to every one of us. Even if you have been a Christian for years, and have had a close walk with the Lord, this heart condition can creep up on you. So, let's look at what it really is in Mark 4: 18-19 (NASB) *"And others are the ones on whom seed was sown among the thorns. These are the ones who have heard the Word, but the worries of the world, the deceitfulness of riches, and the desire for other things enter in and choke the Word and it becomes unfruitful."*

If you have planted and nurtured plants, you know that when you have good rich soil, anything can grow there. Hard-to-grow seeds and common weeds all flourish in good rich soil. So, this heart condition is productive.

Remember that the fruit of this Word crop is "faith." When you have faith in all that God says, your life is productive. You see His plans for you coming into fruition. So, the enemy of your soul will want to fight you in three areas. He will work overtime trying to plant weeds in your garden to ensure that your growth is either stunted or affected by other negative things which we will consider below.

## THE FIRST WEED:
## WORRIES OF THE WORLD.

Let's face it. All of us have problems. We can be rocking along and suddenly there's a health scare, an accident, an unruly family member, or a financial setback. Everyone has those problems. So, what do we do when those setbacks appear? Often, we worry, wiring our hands in despair. We stop looking to the Word, or even praising God, then we cry and moan. And while we are doing that, we start saying or doing all sorts of things which allow weeds to grow in our garden.

Or what about this?

## THE SECOND WEED:
## DECEITFULNESS OF RICHES

Remember when Jesus said that you can't serve God and Mammon Matthew 6:24 (NASB)? The enemy, Satan, wants us to look to money for our answers instead of trusting in God. And, truthfully, it can appear that money solves a lot of problems. Our loving heavenly Father does want us to have enough money for a good life. But money never solves the most important issues in our lives. Happy marriages, happy children, friends, health. None of these things can be bought with money. Nobody needs to be reminded of the rich and famous with wild, unhappy marriages, divorce, drug addictions, rebellious children, and the list goes on. God wants us to be financially blessed. But He doesn't want us to have money as our God. That's when riches become deceitful.

# THE THIRD WEED: LUST FOR OTHER THINGS

What are these other things? Fame, success, romantic pursuits are some of the "other things" which hinder people in their faith walk. We have witnessed ministers with good reputations suddenly fall and be exposed for affairs or sexual perversion. Sometimes alcohol and drug addiction. We have also witnessed ministers who have allowed ambition to sway them from the truth of God's Word. In each of these cases, lust for something else has caused them to falter. Sadly, when these happen, it means that the Word has been choked out by weeds.

So how do we protect ourselves from such detours? From having all those weeds in our hearts? It's simple! We need to look to God and His Word – which will produce faith in us – and produce the results we need in our lives. We don't have to allow our hearts to be swayed by these aberrant desires. Instead, we will have our hearts continually bathed in God's Word and His Spirit. We will also keep our hearts pure before Him – and ask Him to speak to us, letting us know when we are moving in dangerous areas. And, with David we say, "Create in me a clean heart, O God. And renew a right spirit within me"

Psalm 51:10. (NASB) Now this is a time for really sincere soul searching.

Furthermore, you might want to share some of your temptations with others; or you might not want to share. The main thing is to be honest with yourself and with God.

Are you prone to worry? Anger? Negative thoughts? Do you think that money can solve all of your problems? Are you jealous of those who have lots of money? Are you tempted to seek fame? Are you driven by personal success? Do have to fight addiction of any kind? Alcohol? Drugs? Sex? Pornography? Do you have unholy desires for a person?

As you turn to your Father God in repentance, He will restore you. He will also give you the power to overcome these things. Hold them up to Father, and ask for Him to change your heart by the power of His Holy Spirit. Then replace those desires with God's pure Word. Speak the Word. Meditate on it. Declare that Word for you and your family. *"Create in me a clean heart, O God. And renew a right spirit within me." Psalm 51:10 (KJV)*

Having considered the bad soils and their effects, it is time to know which soil is good for planting.

# THE NOBLE AND GOOD HEART— PRODUCES ABUNDANCE

Mark 4:20 (NIV) *"Others, like seed sown on good soil, hear the Word, accept it, and produce a crop – some thirty, some sixty, and some a hundred times what was sown."* This is the last type of soil Jesus mentioned in this parable, is it the good soil. This represents the heart God wants us to have. The heart that will produce. And, what exactly are we producing? We are producing a close walk with God and we are producing faith.

The seed is the Word of God, which creates faith. When we plant it into good, rich soil, it will produce a life of faith. The rocks have been removed – all those hindrances to our walk. We can ignore people's opinions because they don't understand what we are doing when we rely on God and His Word.

Instead of wallowing in people's mockery, we pause God while examining our hearts to take away worry. Alsi, we won't seek only money to solve our problems, and we will be aware of any desires we might have which could distract us. In Luke 8:15 (NIV) *"Account, it says: But the seed on good soil stands for those with a noble and good heart, who hear the Word, retain it, and by persevering produce a crop."*

As we continually till the soil of our hearts in these ways, we can say that we are ready for the Word to produce.

Remember: the seed is God's Word and the crop grows faith in that word, and finally the manifestation of that Word. So, what do you need from God? What do you desire? That's what you plant. Suppose you need healing. You find the healing scriptures, such as, *By the stripes of Jesus, I was healed. Isaiah 53:5 (NIV) or I Peter 2:24 (NIV)*

Or maybe you need finances. *"And my God will meet all of your needs according to the riches of His glory." Phil. 4:19 (NIV)* Or your children might be going through a rebellious spot. *"All your children will be taught by the Lord, and great will be their peace." Isaiah 54:13 (NIV)*

In her book, *Forever Upward,* Suellen Estes gives an account of an experience she had with the Lord. As she was praying and reading the 13th chapter of Matthew, she had a little vision. A mini picture. Matthew 13:44 (NIV) *"The Kingdom of Heaven is like treasure hidden in a field. When a man found it, he hid it again, and then in his joy, he went away and sold all that he had, and bought that field."*

Before that time, Estes had thought of a field with a treasure chest hidden in it. But this was different. She saw a farmer's field which had been freshly planted. There were rows and rows of dirt mounded up where the seed was planted, but not one single sprig of green. No green anywhere. As she pondered this picture, she knew what the Lord was saying.

That's the way it is when we have a major issue in our lives, and start believing in God for transformation, whether it is in our health, our marriages, our children, our finances, anything of great concern.

Indeed, it takes time for seed to produce, so when we first plant this seed, there is no evidence it is even there. A farmer knows that his planted field will produce a beautiful, rich harvest. He has great joy in having a planted field. He continues to care for it. Weeding it. Watering it. Eventually it will produce. If someone tries to discourage him by pointing out the bare dirt, he isn't discouraged. He sells every other idea concerning that field. It's his field. He has planted it. In due season, there will be an awesome crop. That's the way God wants us to be with His Word.

We should see our hearts as that field. When we start planting the Word, we may see nothing at first. But if we keep planting the Word, and we keep watering it, and removing the weeds, we will see a harvest. That's why the Luke version adds *"with perseverance."* If you really want to have the great harvest God wants for you, you will have to be patient.

When you are believing for some big issues in your life, there will be lots of evidence that your faith isn't working. The devil will see to that. He wants you to stop believing God and His Word. But if you will "sell" all of that negative evidence and buy that field, you will see the result.

God's Word is true. And as He helps us plant it in our hearts. He gives us the ability to receive what He has promised us.

As a reminder, consider *Mark 4:26-29 (NIV)* which says, *"This is what the kingdom of God is like. A man scatters seed on the ground. Night and day, whether the man sleeps or gets up, the seed sprouts and grows, though he does not know how. All by itself, the soil produces grain – first the stalk, then the head, then the full kernel in the head. As soon as the grain is ripe, he puts the sickle into it because the harvest has come."*

We don't know how the seed grows, but we know that it does. Just as the natural seed has a genetic code which causes it to produce the crop for which it is designed, we know that God's Word is a seed which produces after its kind. We don't know – and we don't have to know how this happens. All we need to know is that it does. So, find that bag of seeds you need at the moment, and begin planting.

As you begin to plant, purpose in your heart that you are not going to stop until you see the harvest. Never give up. Commit that you are never, ever going to give up! Just continue planting more seeds. As you Speak the Word God has given you, you will see those prayers answered. You will see God working in your life in a greater way than ever!

Now as you close the study, make notes of some ah-ha moments you have received. Share some scriptures which have especially spoken to you. List some areas of your life where you want to grow.

Moreso, as you concentrate on one at a time, find the scriptures which speak to that problem or desire, and begin to claim those for yourself. Read and speak the scriptures daily. Think about them as you go about your day. Ask God to enlighten you more about the meaning of those scriptures. Pray and ask the Holy Spirit to give you more scriptures to back up what you are believing God for. Now you have the Faith Code. May God continue to add years to your life and life to your years. Live a life of unmeasurable abundance!

Made in the USA
Middletown, DE
23 October 2023

41313117R00044